Dear God's Daughter

Words of True Love When False Love Fails

Tonya Raymond

Illustrated by Andry Ismara

Dear:

God's |Daugh.ter|
|dôdər,ˈdädər|noun

1. A human female having the relation of a child to a parent

For in Christ Jesus you are all sons [and daughters] of God, through faith.

- Galatians 3:26 ESV (words in italics my own)

CONTENTS

Who are you?

Run the race...

I will mend your heart...

My gifts to you...

Who I am...

A new season...

My best...

Preface

My Testimony

This can't be it. It can't be over!

Those were the words that kept playing in my mind over and over again when my boyfriend told me via text that he was calling it quits on our relationship.

Trying to process what was happening, I remember suffering from a panic attack while, at the same time, trying to convince him to change his mind.

But he wouldn't let me. He refused to hear me out.

I eventually moved on from trying to fix the relationship and settled for being friends instead (yes, my idea).

I knew it was going to be hard. But I didn't think it was going to be THAT hard! I mean, how do you heal from the person that broke your heart and talk to them on a regular basis as well? For some strange reason, though, I thought I could make it work. I just needed to convince my heart there was still hope. And I needed to tell my brain the same message.

Unfortunately, I was a terrible liar, and the two most damaged organs in my body rejected my botched friendship. My heart and my brain were failing and that's when I knew I needed to take a break.

I felt weird. It was like I was living outside of my body. I wasn't eating. I wasn't doing much of anything. I was simply just existing.

But somehow, I had just enough strength to run to Jesus.

I got on my knees and started to pray (I'm pretty sure a lot more tears came out than actual words).

I cried, fasted, prayed, and worshiped, and repeated this cycle for days. I was searching for Jesus and I wasn't going to stop until I found Him— until I touched Him. I knew deep down He was the only one who could take my pain away.

I would continuously ask, "Why does this keep happening? Is there something wrong with me?"

Somehow, I turned those doubts in my mind into facts: *There has to be something wrong with me. I keep getting used and people keep taking advantage of me.*

My thoughts were tearing me apart. I hated the heart that I had. I hated who I was.

So, I pleaded. I pleaded with Jesus to take away my kind nature. I pleaded with Him to take away my heart.

And then, He responded:

"There is nothing wrong with you. I love you."

It was so audible. It was so clear. It was so Him.

His voice was loud, but at the same time I knew no one else in my house heard Him. His voice was only for me. His voice came from my heart.

Yes, my heart spoke and I knew it was Jesus.

I immediately broke down.

It's weird; in the midst of my tears, I felt great peace. If I had died right then and there, I knew I would've been in His hands.

The love I felt was pure, yet overwhelming. But it was the kind of love that I needed. I've always had the love of my parents—but this, this was different.

A few days later, I felt God led me to research the word "narcissist." I have to admit, I had never really paid attention to that word until that very moment.

As I researched, I questioned, "Was this really my ex?" I dismissed what I read. But it didn't take long for me to discern the truth. God showed me the man I was with. He showed me his heart. It was at that very moment I realized I had just come out of a mentally and emotionally abusive relationship.

I realized that the stolen money, the ghosting, the devaluing, the lies, the women online, the constant emotional withdrawals, the replacement, and the discarding were all signs of being in an abusive relationship.

And that's when I made the decision: I decided to put myself first. I blocked all forms of communication with my ex-boyfriend and never looked back. I chose me. And it felt good!

I decided, also, to put my trust in God. Though it wasn't easy, it was His love that motivated me to heal—I healed with Him and through Him. I was determined to see myself through His eyes, and to give myself the much-needed grace in order to go through my healing journey.

My "Why"

Writing this devotional was hard, to say the least. I doubted myself many times, from questioning if I could even write a book to then asking myself if anyone would read it. I wanted to quit, but God wouldn't let me.

He purposely brought women to me—women who have, at one point or another, been in unhealthy relationships, and women who are still struggling in this area today.

As I began to share my story, I realized I wasn't alone in my experience. According to the National Coalition Against Domestic Violence, 48.4% of women have experienced at least one psychologically-aggressive type of behavior by an intimate partner. The National Domestic Violence Hotline reports that 25% of women in the United

States over 18 years of age have been a victim of severe physical violence by an intimate partner in their lifetime. And in Canada, compared to men, women who have experienced spousal violence are twice as likely to report being sexually assaulted, beaten, choked, or threatened with a gun or knife, according to the Canadian Centre for Justice Statistics.

Social media also became a source of inspiration, and helped me remember my "why." Every so often I would see Instagram posts encouraging me to finish my book and to fulfill my mission.

In that moment I knew I had an obligation to share my story with women, and men, too. I needed to let them know God not only cares about what we go through, but He is able to set us free. He wants to show you just how much He loves you, and that there is nothing wrong with you. He increased my self-confidence, taught me how to love myself, and showed me what His will for my life is. I'm here to tell you He can do the same for you!

*Note: If you need help or are in danger, please contact the National Domestic Violence Hotline at 1-800-799-7233.

How I Did It

To the best of my ability, I laid out the chapters in my book based on how God walked me through my personal healing journey.

Journaling became my therapy, a practice that allowed me to fully release the emotions I held deeply in my heart. I wrote down questions I had for God, and then recorded the answers I received after prayer.

I would highly recommend journaling while on your healing journey, as it serves as a great tool for tracking your progress. Once you feel better, however, please don't make the same mistake I did—don't throw away your notes! I threw out my raw and gut-wrenching words. But, before I threw them out, well, I ripped them up first. At the time, I didn't want to be reminded of the pain that I went through. If only I had waited a few more months; but at the time, writing this book was not on my radar. Let me tell you, though, how I got my notes back. Let me tell you how good God is.

I prayed for God to take me back to my hurtful place, the place of pain I was in right after I was told my relationship was over. Thank God for Jesus! He brought me back! And I truly believe He did that because there was purpose. How did I know

I was back? I felt the pain. It was real again—so real that tears started to roll down my face. And I remembered word-for-word, specific things my ex had said to me—things that I had forgotten. I was broken again. But God healed me—once again.

The chapter, "Ashamed," is written from the perspective of my friend who, at the time, I believed, was in an unhealthy relationship. Supporting a friend in an unhealthy relationship is never easy and, unfortunately, our friendship did not survive. "Ashamed" is about what I believed she was going through based on how our friendship ended, combined with my personal experience in dealing with the emotion of shame.

Healing is weird—it's weird because it's never linear. We can flip-flop from anger to worthlessness to self-blame, and then back to anger. We can feel as though we are healed, but then experience emotional triggers which bring everything to the forefront again. I know this still happens to me, even today. But thank God for His grace and mercy!

God Spoke to Me Through:

His Word: The Bible played an important role in my healing. As I started to read and apply the scriptures to my life, I realized just how much power the Bible holds. The Bible is not just a book. It is the book!

God's Word gave me hope—it gave me life. His words are alive, even today!

Worship: It seemed like every time I attended my home church, the choir chose songs that were hand-picked by Jesus Himself! Every word sung pulled on the strings of my heart and allowed me to feel God's presence.

Men and Women of God: He led me to watch online sermons of prominent men and women of God.

Books: Jesus Calling played a vital role in setting the stage for me to hear from the Son of the living God. I read this devotional book daily before hearing directly from Him.

My Purpose: From a young age, I loved to write, and pursued journalism as a career. I have been a freelance writer for as long as I can remember, but not for one second did I picture myself becoming an author.

He also used my weakness and made it my strength. I thought for a long time that having a caring heart was always going to put me at a disadvantage.

But I had no idea God would position me to help countless women, and to turn my pain into purpose!

Other Thoughts

Although the words in this book align with the Word of God, this book was never meant to replace His Word. But because my words align with His, I knew Jesus was with me throughout my entire book-writing process and healing journey.

And even though this is my story, I wrote it in a way where the reader, God's daughter, can see herself and picture how Jesus might respond.

I also acknowledge you may not relate to each chapter, or that there may be certain areas that God might want you to work on that are not mentioned in this book. Go with what He tells you and shows you through Jesus, and continue your own healing journey with Him.

This book is not meant for everyone. God already knows who this is for.

Dear Heavenly Father,

I thank you so much for placing this book into the hands of your daughter.

I know as she gets ready to embark on this healing journey that you will not only guide her through it, but that you will be with her every step of the way.

I pray that as she sees her true reflection, she will begin to change her lens and see herself through your eyes.

I pray your wisdom, love, and encouragement found throughout these pages will minister to her broken pieces as you piece her back together again.

I pray this book will fuel your daughter's desire to get to know you more by reading and studying your Holy Word and creating a deeper relationship with you.

If there is a history of unhealthy relationships, or even if this is the first one that she has experienced, I ask that you break the strongholds over her life.

I declare she is free and healed even before this journey begins. In Jesus' mighty name, amen.

I know it hurts...

\con.fused\

| kən-ˈfyüzd | adjective

1. *being disordered or mixed up*

Can someone please tell me what just happened?
Was it something I did?

(I can't breathe.)

I mean, this has to be a joke, right?
It just has to be.

Because deep down inside,
I know he still loves me.

(I really can't breathe.)

My heart is racing.
Why won't it stop beating so fast?

(I don't get it.)

This is the relationship I prayed for.
So why is he breaking up with me?

I thought—
I thought God loved me.

(I
just
don't
get it.)

Why is this happening?

Why is this happening now?

Dear Daughter,

I can hear your thoughts.

You have so many questions
but you're not sure where to start.

Please know this is not what I had in mind for you.

It was never my will
to see you hurt or confused.

Whisper my name, and
I will give you what you need.

What you need right now is
peace.

This is your first gift
from me to you,
as you will need this peace—
my peace in order to see you through.

Whisper my name
again, and again,

and watch your heart start to beat
normally again.

Now that your heartbeat's under control,
it's time to focus on your breathing.

As you breathe in, concentrate.

And imagine my breath
filling your lungs.

Inhale.
Exhale.
Trust me, the anxiety will stop.

I know what you're thinking:
if I truly loved you
then why did I allow this to happen?

Daughter, I was desperately trying to reach you.
But you couldn't hear me.

You
refused
to
hear
me.

I allowed this breakup to happen
because I love you.

I couldn't allow this relationship
to go on any longer,

for I knew how it would end
even long before you did.

And I knew how it would end,
if I didn't end it when I did.

I have an obligation to protect you.
I want to make sure that you are safe.

I know you won't understand,
but in time, you will see.

No one can pluck you from my hands
because YOU belong to me.

I know it's asking a lot right now,
but I need you to trust me.

You see, daughter,
I stepped in at this very moment
because you don't know your worth.

For God is not the author of confusion, but of peace, as in all churches of the saints.

- 1 Corinthians 14:33 KJV

Isaiah 30:21   Jeremiah 29:11   Genesis 2:7

\worth.less\

| ˈwərth-ləs | adjective

1. *without worth; of no use, importance, or value; good for nothing*

I stand in front of the mirror, and what do I see?
Someone so low, disgusting, and cheap.

That's what I see.

I always give my all in my relationships,
but it never works out.

It seems like I'm never good enough.
Why am I never enough?

He was emotionless when we broke up.
Cold, distant, heartless.

He heard me falling,
falling apart.

Yet he did nothing.
He said nothing.

He simply refused to talk.

Did he not see his missed calls?
And all those text messages I sent?

The absolute worst feeling in the world
is being left in the dark,
and your messages ignored.

But this wasn't the first time
he's left me high and dry.
You see, ghosting was a regular thing
when it came to him and I.

I pick up my phone
to find multiple notifications.

He liked all my pictures on Instagram;
it must be to get my attention.

I go to his page
to do the same in return;

however, I see a picture of him
and a girl.

(I think I'm going to be sick.)

He just updated his caption: they're boyfriend and
girlfriend.

(I am going to be sick.)

How could he move on so quickly?

Was he with her all this time?

It's as if he enjoys messing with my mind.

Yes,
he's messing with my mind.

I sit here and wonder
how he could treat me this way.

Maybe because I am nothing,
worth nothing.

"Damaged goods" must be printed
on my forehead.

I close my eyes and picture myself jumping
into the endless blue sea.

It's like I'm on a cliff and tiny rocks are

f
a
l
l
i
n
g

from beneath my feet.

I replay in my mind the beautiful words
he said to me one gloomy afternoon:

"It's you that I want, no one else.
You're everything to me."

Then six months later, he told me that he loved me.

He said it only once, once when he was drunk.

And that's when I opened my eyes.

Lies.

Lies.

Lies.

Was it all just lies?

So, back to the cliff I go.
The cliff I envisioned in my mind.

All I can think about now is who's going to love me,
love me enough to catch me when I fall?

I am drowning,
sinking in my thoughts.
And he knows I can't swim.

But I jump anyway,
into the deep blue sea.

Dear Daughter,

For every negative thought you have,
it's like a thousand knives aimed at your soul.

That's why it's so important to control your thoughts
and listen to my words:

There is NOTHING wrong with you.

AB-SO-LUTE-LY NOTHING.

You say no one will ever love you.

But I LOVE YOU.

I LOVE YOU.

You are not worthless,
because you mean everything to me.

And you are much more valuable
than the birds nesting in the trees.

Don't allow other voices to seep into your mind;
amongst all the chatter, just search for mine.

Mine is the most beautiful voice that your spirit will
ever know.
And once you find it, allow my words to penetrate
your soul.

I love you.

I love you.

I love you.

You could never sink so low
or fall so fast that you would hit rock bottom.

After all, look around—
can't you see that I've caught you?

Don't panic. I'm here.

I am right here.

In my loving hands you are safe,
and where you need to be.

Even with those broken pieces,
your heart is still in sync with mine.

You are safe—
perfectly safe,

for I am with you.
And you will never be alone.

She is much more precious than rubies; nothing you desire can compare with her.

– Proverbs 3:15 NIV

Hebrews 4:15   Matthew 6:26   Psalm 118:13-14

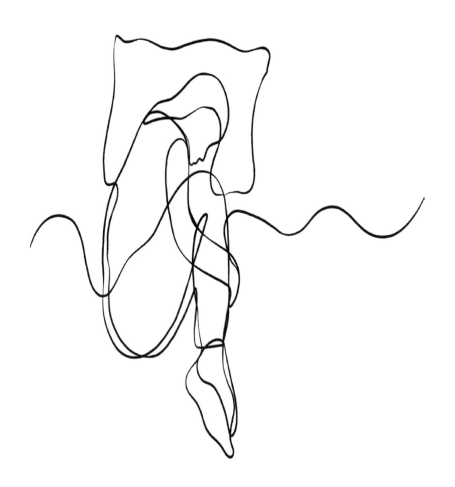

\ a. lone \
| ə-ˈlōn | adjective

1. having no one else present

I don't think You understand.

You took my world away

MY
WHOLE
WORLD!

Who am I supposed to talk to?
Or laugh with when I find something funny?

What's the point of anything anymore,
now that I'm all alone and lonely?

I grew up hearing the saying,

"God will never leave you.
He will never forsake you."

So then, where are You?
WHERE ARE YOU WHEN I NEED YOU?

Don't You hear your daughter crying?
Can't You see how much pain I'm in?

Why can't You just change his mind?

Please,
change his mind.

I don't want to be alone.

I don't know how to be alone.

I'm scared.

Dear Daughter,

I know you think you're all alone
now that the person who meant the world to you is
gone.

But I need you to know that you are my whole world.
And I will never forsake you.

How can I be so sure?

Well, you see, your future isn't scary
because I went before you to secure it.

I know all the bumps, the highs, and the lows.
I know it so well that I can guide you through it.

I am always beside you.
So, whatever you feel, I feel it too.

Trust me when I say this:
I know what it's like to be alone too.

In the last few days of my life,
I was in agony and my disciples were asleep.

I cried out to my Father,
but I could not hear Him speak.

So, when you speak,
just know I understand the depth of your words.

And when you can only cry,
just know I understand the tears that you shed.

And when you have no more tears to shed,
just know I understand—
I understand what you can no longer give.

And lastly, daughter, I am behind you:
behind you to push, and to remind you
to keep going even when you feel like giving up.

You will never truly be alone,
because I will be your protector.

In this world people will disappoint you,
turn their backs on you at a moment's notice.

But even when you stray,
my hands will always remain open.

Just call on me
and you'll know I'm near.

For I am with you, with you always.

There's no need to blame yourself—
this is not your fault.

Don't be afraid, for I am with you. Don't
be discouraged, for I am your God. I will
strengthen you and help you. I will hold you
up with my victorious right hand.

- Isaiah 41:10 NLT

Psalm 139:16   Matthew 26:39-40   Revelation 21:4

(self)\ blame \

| ˈblām | verb

1. To find fault with

But maybe this is my fault.
I was too emotional;
I scared him off.

I used to tell him how I felt.

How much I loved him.
How much I missed him.

I think I might have told him too much—
that it overwhelmed him.

I should have stayed silent.
If I had a chance it do it all over again, I would.

I would have shut off my emotions,
and chosen my words more carefully.

Space.

I would give him more space.

That's why he ghosted.
Yes, I'm the one to blame.

Dear Daughter,

This is not your fault.
So please don't go down that terrible path.
Don't pick yourself apart.

I created you to be you,
emotional and all.

I created you to feel,
to have an opinion.

So, don't get so down on yourself
that you can no longer hear my voice.

Self-blame is toxic;
it will erode your mind and then your soul.

It's a losing battle when you start
believing the lies you are told.

So, to fix this, transfer your cares and burdens onto
me,
for I need you to look at things differently
in order to see what I see.

There are givers, and unfortunately there are takers,
my daughter.
He wanted to take who you were,
who I created you to be.

Don't you see what was happening?
You had thoughts of changing your true being.

There is nothing more you can do

when a relationship becomes this unhealthy.

But if you spend time with me, I will show you
his heart and his true intention.

You two created what's called a soul tie;
a tie which was never meant to be formed.

But fear not, daughter;
I will show you how to break this bond.

It requires a lot of work,
as you need total dependence on me.

I will show you the things you missed.
And tell you what you simply couldn't hear.

In the body of his flesh through death,
to present you holy and unblameable and
unreproveable in his sight:
- Colossians 1:22, KJV

1 Corinthians 7:17   John 10:27   Psalm 55:22

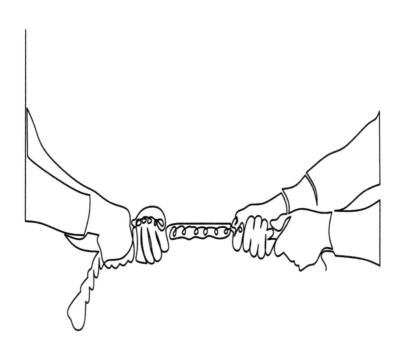

\ soul \
| ˈsōl | noun

1. the principle of life, feeling, thought, and actions in humans, regarded as a distinct entity separate from the body, and commonly held to be separable in existence from the body; the spiritual part of humans as distinct from the physical part.

\ tie \
| ˈtī | transition verb

1. to bind, fasten, or attach with a cord, string, or the like; drawn together and knotted

I don't know if I can break away from him.
I don't think I'm strong enough.

I can't seem to get him out of my mind.
I feel so attached—
addicted, like to a drug.

I know he's not good for me,
but I think I want him back.

Even after all the hurt.
Even after all the pain.

I'm just not going to let a year and a half simply go to
waste.

If he hasn't changed, then I can change him.
I can make him love me again.

I just have to try harder.
And then just maybe
it will last.

So, I can handle this break, Jesus.
I can take the loss.

Just as long as You place us back together one day,
then all might not be lost.

Dear Daughter,

There are good ties, and bad ones.
Some I formed, and some you formed without me.

You were tied to the wrong one
and formed this bond prematurely.

You made him yours
through the words that you spoke

and formed a bond through
the intimacy you shared.

But what you failed to realize
is that what you do and say impacts the spiritual
realm.

A soul tie can be great, producing endless fruit.
Or it can be unhealthy, bearing spoiled, rotten fruit,

sowing seeds of doubt and confusion—
all of which you are experiencing now.

This soul you are connected to was meant to drain
and deplete you.

It was meant to keep you in total bondage.
It was meant to drown and kill you.

Yes, he spoke about me, but never truly loved me.
Yet you made him your idol and decided to put him
above me.

You wear a mask every day.

Every day, I see you.

You cry yourself to sleep every night.
Every night, I hear you.

This relationship has robbed you of more than you
could even imagine.
It has robbed you of me.

Yet you struggle to let him go.
It's the soul tie, you see.

But fear not, daughter; this can be undone.
I am the God of restoration and I will break this bond.

You will have everything that was ever stolen from
you.
You can have it all back.

There is freedom
in saying goodbye.

Now when he had finished speaking to Saul,
the soul of Jonathan was knit to the soul of
David, and Jonathan loved him as his own soul

- 1 Samuel 18:1 NKJV

Proverbs 18:21   Matthew 18:18   Luke 6:43-45

Come to me...

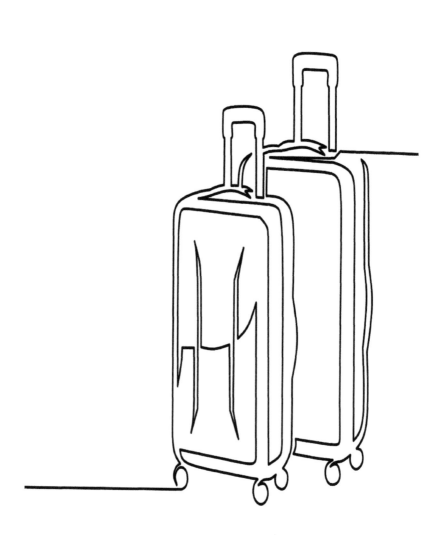

\good.bye\

|gu̇d-ˈbī| noun

1. a taking of leave

It's time to say goodbye.

Goodbye to the man I thought I knew,
and to the relationship I once cherished.

Goodbye to the laughs,
to the adoration,
and the love bombing.

Goodbye to the lies,
the isolation,
and the sleepless nights.

Goodbye to the mind games,
the constant manipulation,
the put downs, and the devaluing.

Goodbye to the ghosting,
and the gaslighting,
the walking on eggshells too.

Goodbye to the selfishness,
the soul withdrawals,
and the constant suffering.

I wish I had said it sooner,
but nevertheless, I'm saying it now.

Goodbye to the man I thought I loved.
Goodbye for good.

This will not be a repeated cycle,
not with everything You have shown me.

I've finally done it!
Blocked and discarded.

But tell me—why, Jesus, do I feel so ashamed?

"Then you will know the truth, and the truth will set you free."

- John 8:32 NIV

Ecclesiastes 3:6   Proverbs 4:25   Isaiah 43:18-19

Don't run...

\ a. shamed \
|ə-ˈshāmd| adjective

1. embarrassed or guilty because of one's actions, characteristics, or associations

Dear Jesus,

How could I be so blind?

How could I not see it for what it was—
see him for who he was?

I mean, everyone saw right through the facade.
My friends, my family, even my mom.

They tried to warn me,
but I didn't listen.

I lost some of the closest people in my life.

He told me they were negative
and needed to be removed from my life.

Deep down, I knew it wasn't true,
but I went along with it anyway.

I took offence to anything that was said
that challenged my fantasy,
my lie,
my truth.

I became cold and distant towards the ones I loved.

It's funny,
I became the one that broke my own heart.

That's why I'm so ashamed.

I wish I could tell them what happened,
and explain how I am truly feeling.

How much I miss them.
How much I love them.
How much I'm truly sorry.

But I can't.

I'd rather just kill those friendships,
and family relationships as well.

To make myself better, I'll justify it
first to myself, then to them, and then somehow to
You.

I'll end it via text.

Yes, that's what I will do.

I know it will hurt them
because, well, this hurts me too.

But it's better this way.
They must never know how ashamed I am.

I mean, look at how I treated them!

Why would they want anything to do with me?

I mean, I don't want anything to do with me.

I let them down. I let You down.

I am so ashamed.

Dear Daughter,

You have everything to gain when you start living in truth.

And once you see your guilt through my eyes, you will know what to do.

Mending relationships takes humility and courage— things I can help you with, so you need not worry.

But, don't put off what you can do right now. Time stops for no one, so it's best to say it now.

Remember, friends and family are there to encourage and to support you.

So, cherish the ones I've put in your life who still care and pray for you.

Some may never come back and some will simply need more time. But be patient and you'll see; everything will work out just fine.

Until then, my child, there is more work for you to do. Let's now look at your anger and see how that is controlling you.

Do not be afraid; you will not be put to shame. Do not fear disgrace; you will not be humiliated. You will forget the shame of your youth and remember no more the reproach of your widowhood.

- Isaiah 54:4 NIV

John 8:32   Colossians 3:13   Proverbs 27:10

\an.ger\

| ˈaŋ-gər | noun

1. *a strong feeling of displeasure and belligerence aroused by a wrong*

I'm sorry Jesus, but I can't seem to let it go.

How could he do this to me and destroy my soul?

He knew how I felt, how I felt about him,

yet all he ever did was hurt me
over and over again.

You don't do that to someone—
not someone you love.

Do You know what it feels like to realize your relationship
wasn't built on love?

Lies.

It was built on lies,
and survived on it too.

To know it wasn't real
hurts.

And now I want to hurt him
just as much.

Because he stole. He stole
so much from me.

Not only material things.
But he stole my peace,
my joy, my sanity.

My happiness and my light.

My heart.

Yes, he damaged my soul.

So, tell me why he should get away with it?

He showed no remorse.
None.

He showed no emotions.
Not even one.

Is he even human?
Does he have a heart to feel?

I'm holding on to all this anger.

And it's slowly killing me.

It is slowly killing
my peace,
my joy,
my sanity.

Dear Daughter,

I know the things he did to you,
and trust me—they will not go unaccounted.

You know I am very protective of you, my love,
and the others I call my own.

So, leave him to me.
Let's shift the focus onto you—

it's time to discuss the anger
that is controlling you.

It is very dangerous, darling, to leave anger
unchecked
because there is always the potential to act on it.

It is a strong emotion
that the enemy will use to plant seeds
and poison your soul.

Yes, anger can lead you to dark places—
places you might not wish to go.

I know it isn't easy,
but I will need you to find me
as soon as an evil thought crosses your mind.

Call out to me, read my Word.
And you will be filled with my light.

You will need to do this many times
until you are back in control.

Then, I will need you to pray for the one who
damaged your soul.

Pray that he may find me,
and that he may change his ways.

Pray to free yourself of anger, my darling.
You don't want to make yourself sick.

Dear friends, never take revenge. Leave that to the righteous anger of God. For the Scriptures say, "I will take revenge; I will pay them back," says the Lord.

- Romans 12:19 NLT

Ephesians 4:26-31   Matthew 5:44   Psalm 38:3

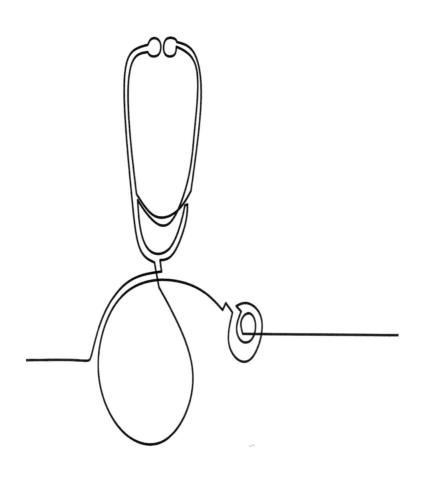

\ self-med.i.ca.tion \

|ˌself-ˌme-di-ˈkā-shən| noun

1. The act or process of medicating oneself especially without the advice of a physician

I need something to take the pain away.
Something that can ease the hurt for just a little bit.

I should go shopping.

Or maybe I should change my hairstyle?
I mean, I always wanted it shorter anyway.

I'll take some pictures and post it on Instagram.
I'm guaranteed to get praise then.

Or what if I get dressed up and go on a date?
I'll get the attention I need as well.

But then again,
it's all superficial.

What's the point,
when I'm not truly happy?

So tell me, Jesus.
Tell me: what else can I do?

What else can I do
to take the pain away
for just a little bit?

What can be prescribed
for a broken heart like mine?

Dear Daughter,

Self-medicating the pain will only mask the problem.
It will only give you temporary relief.

But I have the power to set you free once and for all
and give you what you so desperately need.

You'll need to surrender those areas to me.
Yes, those voids too.

Next, you'll need to speak victory over yourself,
when the devil comes to tempt you.

Flee from him and come to me,
and the urge to self-medicate will dissipate—

for I have created a plan, a way out.
But it's your job to recognize it and follow through.

So, how do you set yourself free, you ask?

First, you confess.
Then practice forgiveness.

He heals the brokenhearted and binds up their wounds.

- Psalm 147:3 NIV

Mark 2:17   John 8:36   1 Corinthians 10:13

Take what you need...

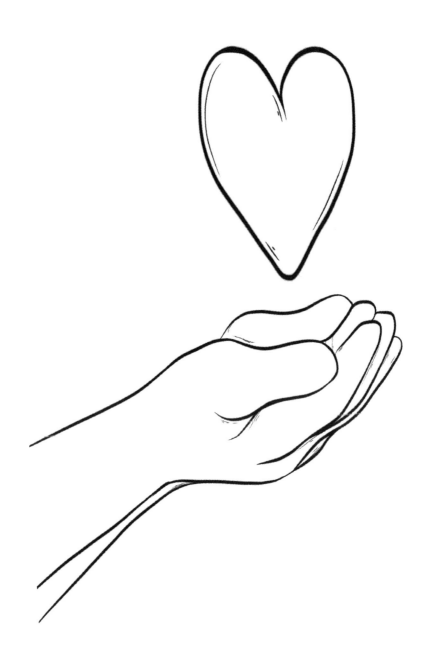

\for.give.ness\

|fər-ˈgiv-nəs| noun

1. the attitude of someone who is willing to forgive

Okay, Jesus. I prayed for him,
but now You want me to forgive?

And not only do You want me to forgive him,
but You want me to forgive myself as well?

I mean, I can try to forgive him in time. I guess.

But forgiving myself?
That's something I simply cannot do.

I stood by and let him hurt me.
I mean,
I literally watched
as he set out to destroy.

I was the one that slid into his DMs
and initiated a conversation.

I saw all the signs and red flags,
but proceeded anyway.

And once I had him—
the relationship I wanted—
I begged You to bless it.

When it got tough,
I saw more flags pop up,
but I still didn't feel like it was time to give him up.

I pleaded with You—to keep it going.

But it came to an end,
I blamed You for it.

Do you know what it's like to be attached to someone
with bad intentions?

I hate what he's done to me.
And I hate him for making me hate myself.

So, no, I don't deserve forgiveness.
I don't deserve to forgive myself.

Because I did this—I did all of this.
I did this to myself.

Dear Daughter,

You are holding yourself at an impossible mark.
That's something that should only be left to me.

Unlike what you're doing now—I forgive.
And forgive and forgive and forgive.

You've been forgiven, from the moment you asked.
You've been set free but you don't even know it.

Why hurt yourself even more?
Why self-inflict your pain?

It is a grim and hurtful path you're on, my child,
when you start to condemn yourself and are blind to
the truth.

Come out from the enemy's lies and see what I see.

You need to realize, my darling, forgiveness is for
everyone—
even for you.

Forgive, and forgive, and forgive.
Then start all over again and forgive.

It will get easier—trust me.
It will get easier because of my love.

Therefore, there is now no condemnation for those who are in Christ Jesus.

- Romans 8:1 NIV

John 5:22   Isaiah 43:25   Matthew 6:14-15

\ love \
| ˈləv | noun

1. a feeling of strong or constant affection for a person

I thought love was receiving texts throughout the day,
even when he refused to see me.

I thought it was receiving gifts
every time he knew that he was guilty.

I thought it was making him happy,
even when he didn't do the same in return.

I thought love was saying yes,
even when I didn't want to give him a loan.

I thought it was going above and beyond
to prove my undying love—

to prove to him I was not like the others
that failed to show him love.

I thought it was giving my all—
mind, body, and soul—in order to make him commit.

Never did I think he would one day
just get up and quit.

I thought love was putting my wants and desires on
hold.
And never telling others the secrets and lies that he
told.

I thought it meant we were Bonnie and Clyde.
It was supposed to be just me and him;
I was his ride or die.

I thought love was control and protection,
mixed with a bit of jealousy.
Never once did I think I'd be trading in my happiness

to be so low on energy.

I thought it was all those things
because he apologized and said he was sorry.

He said it was in the name of love—
he did it because he loved me.

I thought he loved me.

I thought I loved me.

What is love?

Dear Daughter,

Love is what I founded the Earth upon. Then I noticed my children were in trouble—and that's why I chose to die on the cross.

Love is action—
an action of sacrifice.
It means much more than simply recited words.

It was never meant to be twisted,
or selfish.

Manipulated,
or something you earned.

It is to be given freely,
without expectation.

For you see, love can't be measured;
it simply cannot be contained.

Love is who I Am.
And you can't know true love without me.

When you accept my love,
then, and only then, you will begin to see how I see.

Not blinded by fame, material things, or wealth,
but by patience, grace, and understanding.

It is a force that is so mighty and powerful
that it can build up anyone that was once down.

It can remove pain. It can heal and restore you.
Yes, love—my love is that profound.

Love is patient, love is kind. It does not envy, it does not boast, it is not proud. It does not dishonor others, it is not self-seeking, it is not easily angered, it keeps no record of wrongs. Love does not delight in evil but rejoices with the truth. It always protects, always trusts, always hopes, always perseveres. Love never fails.

– 1 Corinthians 13:4-8a NIV

John 3:16   Jeremiah 31:3   Ephesians 3:19

\ heal.ing \

| ˈhēl | noun

1. the process of becoming well again, especially after a cut or other injury

I'm not sure when it started.
I'm not sure why things happened the way they did.

I just know that I'm broken.
And I don't know how to feel better again.

I want to be whole.
I really, really do.

So, Jesus can you heal me?
Because I want to heal with You.

Come to me, all you who are weary and burdened, and I will give you rest. Take my yoke upon you and learn from me, for I am gentle and humble in heart, and you will find rest for your souls. For my yoke is easy and my burden is light.

- Matthew 11:28-30 NIV

Psalm 147:3   1 Thessalonians 5:23   Psalm 30:2

(a) \ pro.mised \ (life)
| ˈprä-məs | transition verb

1. pledge to do, bring about, or provide

Dear Daughter,

Because you are ready to heal,
you can have the life I desire for you.

It is a life that I dreamed up
before you even became you.

It is far better
than you could even think of,
but something you'll need training for.

The next few months
will be some of the most challenging times of your
life,

but if you trust me,
I will make it right.

I promise to be with you every step of the way.

I promise to comfort you when the sky above you
turns gray.

I promise to love you through the lonely and scary
times you go through.

I promise you will see hope in everything that I do.

I promise you will reach not only a level of happiness,
but of everlasting joy.

I promise you all of this, my Word will not return void.

But in order for these promises, my darling, to come
to pass,
I will need you to take off your mask.

"For I know the plans I have for you," declares the Lord, "plans to prosper you and not to harm you, plans to give you hope and a future."
- Jeremiah 29:11 NIV

John 16:33   Matthew 28:20   Isaiah 55:11

Who are you?

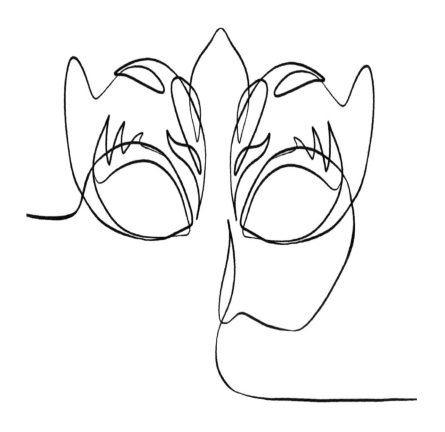

\ mask \

|ˈmask | noun

1. a manner or expression that hides one's true character or feelings

I'm back in front of the mirror,
but this time my mask is cracking.

Where is the glue?

Why can't I find it?

Why can't I fix it?

Sigh.

Too late—a million broken pieces too late.

I look up, glancing in the mirror.
For a split second, I catch my reflection.

Hideous, I thought.
Disgusting came next.

As I cover my face,
I hear a distinct voice.

I know who it is.
I can no longer run from her.

I slowly remove my hands from my face
and take a look into the mirror.

I see a little girl crying—
she looks kind of familiar.

She tries to talk,
but I stop her.

I'm not ready to hear from her.
No, not now.

My heart is breaking because I want to love her.
I simply don't know how.

I want to know who hurt her,
but then I suddenly change my mind.

So, I do what I think is best:
I silence her.

"Forget about it!" I yell to the little girl.
"Move on!" I scream to my reflection.

Wait a minute, did I imagine all of this?
Was it all just in my head?

I wonder what she was trying to tell me,
what she would have told me if I allowed her to
speak.

I have another vision, and then it hits me:
she wanted to answer my question—my question
about who hurt her.

She wanted to say,
it was me.

Can a man hide himself in secret places so that I cannot see him? declares the LORD. Do I not fill heaven and earth? declares the LORD.

- Jeremiah 23:24 ESV

Luke 12:2   Luke 8:17   Proverbs 26:24

(the)\ truth \

| ˈtrüth | noun

1. a verified or indisputable fact

The truth is, I've hurt myself
more than those who've hurt me.

I allowed the words spoken by others
to consume and control me.

The truth is, I believed the lies.

I made excuses and stayed busy.
I sabotaged everything that was good.

The truth is, I run.

I was living a life of sin.
But I never thought it would catch up with me.

The truth is, I am exhausted.

I know You're not happy with my actions.
No, I am not happy either.

But the truth is…
I don't know who I am.

"Then you will know the truth, and the truth will set you free."

- John 8:32 NIV

Romans 12:2   Proverbs 28:1   Numbers 32:23

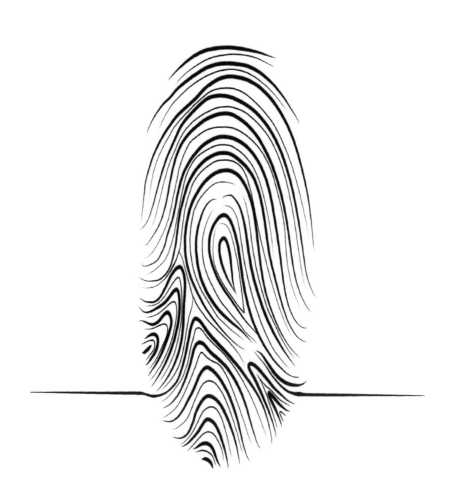

\ i.den.ti.ty \
|ī-ˈden-tə-tē| noun

1. condition or character as to who a person or what a thing is; the qualities, beliefs, etc., that distinguish or identify a person

I was smart, confident,
independent. A go-getter.

I was radiant like the sun—
so full of energy.

But then I met my ex
and that's when things began to change.

Everything I knew about myself
—everything I liked—
just blew up in my face.

Why am I no longer happy?
Why am I even here?

Why did You pick me, God,
when I'm not sure of who I am?

Oh, how I wish my mask didn't break.
How I wish I could piece it back together again.

Every broken piece represented a lie,
a lie that I told myself.

That mask was my everything. Now, what do I really
have?

My self-worth was in that relationship;
my identity he controlled.

Now I'm struggling to breathe,
but am I really living though?

I'm faced with the person that I am,
the person who was left behind.

It's this heart.
Oh, how I wish it wasn't mine.

I don't want to be this person,
who loves so deeply, and repeatedly gets abused.

If You could just take away my emotions,
then it wouldn't be so bad.

Make me over, Jesus,
with what I do not wish to have.

Not with a big heart,
a caring heart that gets misused and trampled on.

Make me cold and heartless just like the one that
made me, me.

Dear Daughter,

You are my child (John 1:12). You are healed (Isaiah 53:5). You are strong (Psalm 18:32). You are forgiven (1 John 2:12). You are adopted (Ephesians 1:5). You are whole (Colossians 2:10). You are mine (Isaiah 43:1). You are not alone (Joshua 1:9). You are victorious (Corinthians 15:57). You are joyful (John 15:11). You are powerful, loved, and have a sound mind (2 Timothy 1:7). You are fearfully and wonderfully made (Psalm 139:14). You are my friend (John 15:15). You are justified and redeemed (Romans 3:24). You are no longer a slave to sin (Romans 6:6). You are free (Galatians 5:1). You are righteous and holy (Ephesians 4:24). You are my workmanship (Ephesians 2:10). You are bought by my blood (Ephesians 2:13). You are a citizen of heaven (Philippians 3:20). You are beautiful (Psalm 45:11). You are unique (Psalm 139:13). You are my daughter (Galatians 3:26). You are favored (Proverbs 8:35). You are made in my image (Genesis 1:27). You are the apple of my eye (Psalm 17:18).

Run the race...

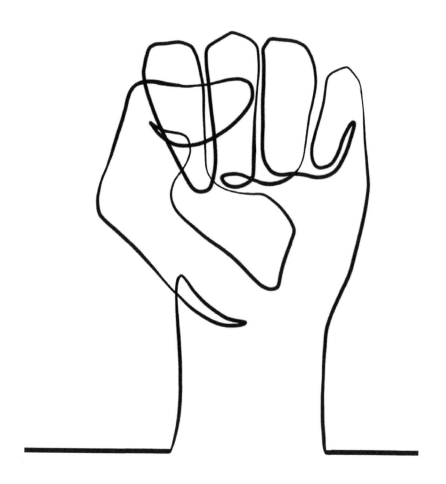

\ strength \

| ˈstreŋ(k)th |, | ˈstren(t)th | noun

1. the emotional or mental qualities necessary in dealing with difficult or distressing situations

Dear Jesus,

I can't do this anymore.

Working on myself requires too much energy, time, and way too much thought.

To face this kind of pain is both mentally and physically exhausting.

I don't have any more strength
in me to face me.

Dear Daughter,

Please don't abort the mission because you lack strength.
Ask for help—I will give you mine instead.

You have something to birth and to give to the world, but you will need my power to bring it to this earth.

So follow my lead, my darling, because this baby is almost due.
I know the labor is painful, but there are so many blessings I want to bestow on you.

When you push through all the pain, you will birth freedom, peace, and love.

Those are the very things that were stolen, but I can give them to you from heaven up above.

It will be better—better than you could even imagine. Just wait and see.

But in order to get there, I need you to push for me.

Prepare your mind, your bundle of joy is on its way.

I need you to think positively every step of the way.

I can do all things through Christ who strengthens me.

- Philippians 4:13 NKJV

Isaiah 41:10   John 16:21   Jeremiah 30:17

(a)\re.new.ed\(mind)
|ri-ˈnü| -ˈnyü verb

1. To make or become new, fresh, or strong again

Jesus,

My thoughts have been mostly negative.
I'm not sure how to escape.

It all seems to start
when I think I've made a mistake.

My heart stops and my mind feels cluttered.
Then I hear a high-pitched voice say,

Look at what you did…this is all your fault!

It's my mind—it's talking again.
It's repeating the same words I used to tell myself
over and over again.

It's like there is a dark cloud above my head.
When I look up, there's no hope.

The cloud opens up.
The rain begins to fall.

"You're a failure."

"What a loser."

"You will never be good enough."

There must be a hole in my head,
because those words keep coming in.

I look around and I just want to sit—
sit in my own self-pity.

Nobody cares.
No one can even begin to understand
that I'm drowning
and I can't get out.

Dear Daughter,

I know you want to get out,
out of the prison that you're in.

But you will never truly escape,
if you don't start renewing
that mind you are living in.

Renewing your mind means
thinking the way that I do—
thinking of you how I think about you.

Not just thinking,
but also believing what I say about you.

I know it won't be easy.

This negative way of thinking
has been ingrained in you for years.

See your mind as a battlefield, my darling.

On one side you have me,
the way to everything good and pure,

and on the other side you have the devil
who is known for his relentless grip.

When you choose to live for me,
the enemy will seek you out.

His mission is clear:
to keep you in bondage
where there is no way out.

In order to be prepared for the attacks that will come,
you must put on the armor that
I designed specifically for you.

Start by fastening the truth around your waist;
study my word day and night.

Then put on your breastplate,
which needs to be in good standing with me.

Next, make sure the shoes of peace fit and are
comfortable enough to stand in.
Remember to grasp the shield of faith tightly when
the enemy begins to attack.

The helmet of salvation is important,
for this is where the enemy likes to appear if your
mind is not well-protected.

Lastly, pick up the sword of the spirit,
for you're fighting not only in the physical realm, but
also in the spiritual.

Now that you have your armor on, wait for further
instructions.

Remember, daughter—I will equip you for every
battle you will face,
including against the dark lies of rejection.

Do not be conformed to this world, but be transformed by the renewal of your mind, that by testing you may discern what is the will of God, what is good and acceptable and perfect.

— Romans 12:2 ESV

Isaiah 55:8-9 Philippians 4:8 Ephesians 6:10-18

I will mend your heart...

\ re.jec.tion\
|ri-ˈjek-shən |noun

1. the act of not giving someone the love and attention they want and expect

It's one thing to be rejected by strangers,
it's another when it's by someone you love.

All my life I wanted acceptance—
I craved belonging.

I thought for sure that we belonged together.
I thought we were going to stay in each other's lives.

But when he rejected me,
it felt like a thousand knives hit the bullseye.

I thought I would be used to it by now.
I have quite a few stab wounds, you see.

But when I came face-to-face with rejection,
those scabs started to open up and bleed.

My heart was bleeding.
My soul was bleeding too.

And those thoughts?
Yep, You guessed it!
They came back too.

If I was enough,
then why did he cut me out of his life?

The moments right after the breakup
became some of the most painful experiences
in my life.

To finally belong.
And then to no longer have a place.

I needed him to love me.
It needed to be him because I
rejected myself a long time ago.

Why do I have to repeatedly deal with rejection,
Jesus?

Why do I have to deal with it now?

Dear Daughter,

Don't you remember I was rejected all my life?
I know what it feels like. I know how much it hurts.

But I'm here to tell you there is good in rejection,
even when it hurts.

My daughter, there was nothing more you could have
done.
It was inevitable that you needed to come back to
me.

So, the next time you are faced with rejection,
I want you to take a few moments to just simply
breathe.

Then picture yourself as a beautiful flower in a flower
store.

There are people coming from far and wide
to pick the ones they love.

They pick ones to the left and to the right of you.

Breathe.

I want you to know that I see you.
I see you.

It's now closing time
and you remain.

Breathe.

I want you to know that
I still see you; I see you.

I will pick you up.
Again, and again.

Because I saw you.
Because I love you.
It's okay now to exhale.

Forget those who walk away.
Learn to praise me.

All rejection simply means is
re-direction back to me.

You have the power to overcome it
because I overcame it first.

But in order for you to survive it,
you need to live in me.

In me is where you are safe.

In me you don't have to work to earn my love.

You are accepted.

Completely and fully in me.

Breathe my darling,
there's no need to feel anxiety.

As you come to him, the living Stone – rejected by humans but chosen by God and precious to him

– 1 Peter 2:4 NIV

Luke 22:54-62   2 Corinthians 12:9   Psalm 94:14

\ anx.i.e.ty\

|aŋ-ˈzī-ə-tē |noun

1. an uncomfortable feeling of nervousness or worry about something that is happening or might happen in the future

I experienced anxiety when he stopped talking to me, and then it got worse when he suddenly left.

My mind felt like a malfunctioned merry-go-round— spinning fast, then out of control.

How did I get here?

What's going to happen next?

Were some of the questions I had spinning in my head.

And my heart? Well, it felt like it was going explode—explode right out my chest!

I thought I was slowly going crazy, and thought for sure a trip to the hospital would be next.

To not have control of your mind and your heart is such a terrible feeling.

And since the breakup? Well, I've experienced more panic attacks and anxiety.

So, Jesus, tell me: how do I fix my anxious thoughts when all I do is worry?

Dear Daughter,

Go to a quiet place
and just sit with me for a while.

Then, just as we practiced,
whisper my name,
and I will help you center yourself.

Train your thoughts to find me
the minute you feel anxious and ready to let go.

Keep searching until you find me.
Remember to breathe as you go.

When you think about everything else—everything
but me—
your thoughts will lead your right into anxiety.

Don't do life without me, darling.
I need you to depend on me.

Cast all your anxiety on him because he cares for you.

- 1 Peter 5:7 NIV

Psalm 37:7   Hebrews 6:19-20   Proverbs 8:17

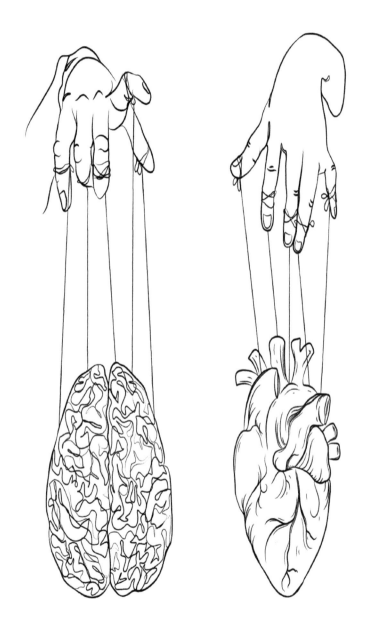

\ co.de.pen.den.cy \
| ˌkō-di-ˈpen-dən(t)-sē |noun

1. a psychological condition or a relationship in which a person manifesting low self-esteem and a strong desire for approval has an unhealthy attachment to another person and places the needs of that person before his or her own

When I like someone,
I tend to fall quickly.

I forget who I am,
and lose myself completely.

Anything he needed, I gave him:
money, attention, emotional support—it was always
there.

When I felt he was disappointed,
I wondered how I could have messed up.

I used to get so upset with myself for always messing
up.

His happiness was my happiness.
It became more important than my own.

I used to worship the ground he walked on
though I hated the person he was inside.

When he would disappear,
it felt as though I was dying.

So, I sought his attention.
I needed it to keep on surviving.

This is how it went
for an entire year and a half.

I was on an emotional rollercoaster,
but I chose not to get off.

I always said:
if it was going to end,
then it had to be from him.

Looking back at it now,
I'm so happy that he did.

Dear Daughter,

I created you to be someone.

Someone who can stand on their own two feet,
but with my support.

Someone who can think for themselves,
but needs me to inspire the right thoughts.

Someone who can be completely whole,
but requires me to be complete.

Someone who can move on their own,
but still needs me to guide them.

You don't have to perform for me to get my
attention.
Because you are always on my mind—
24/7.

I am already drawn to you.
I am madly and deeply in love with you.

All I ask is that you make me the head of your world,
so that I can give you the peace that you need in this
life.

It is better to take refuge in the Lord than to trust in humans.

- Psalm 118:8 NIV

Isaiah 41:10   Colossians 3:2   Psalm 139:17-18

\ peace\
| ˈpēs |noun

1. *a quiet and calm state of mind*

I remember the first words You spoke.
They gave me instant peace.

They were beautiful.
They were real.
They were your first gift to me.

It seemed like time had stopped.
And it felt like I could breathe again.

It was something I was missing in my relationship,
something I never want to be without again.

So, tell me, Jesus, how do I find Your peace once
again?

Dear Daughter,

To find peace is to find me.

And in order to find me,
all you need to do is ask.

I am always ready—ready to rescue you from the
storm.

To calm your thoughts
and to calm your emotions.

It is my peace that will keep you sane, my daughter,
sane in the midst of trouble.

Peace, peace,
my beautiful peace
is what you'll need when you face abandonment.

Peace I leave with you; my peace I give you. I do not give to you as the world gives. Do not let your hearts be troubled and do not be afraid.

- John 14:27 NIV

Isaiah 9:6   Mark 4:39   Psalm 37:39

\ a.ban.don.ment\

|ə-ˈban-dən-mənt| adjective

1. the act of leaving someone or something or ending or stopping something, usually forever

He left me on the side of the road.
Wet, cold, abandoned.

How could someone who says they love you,
treat you like you're garbage?

You hope and pray they would remember,
remember where they left you.

But I was always an afterthought
once he got what he wanted.

He couldn't feel.
But he could see.

He saw where I was placed,
because he put me there.

I was left in the dark, on the side of the road.
Wet, cold, abandoned.

It makes sense why I struggle with this today,
why I distance myself from others.

Because I remember what it is like.

To be left
all alone.

On the side of the road.

Wet, cold, abandoned.

Dear Daughter,

The feeling of abandonment is one of the most
crushing feelings in this world.

It is paired with rejection,
and followed by the state of loneliness.

I know, it is very painful, my darling,
but I need you to remember my words.

No matter what happens to you,
I will never leave you alone.

See me as your permanent shadow.
I am your radiant light in the midst of darkness.
You can run, but you will never outrun me.

I will follow you into the stickiest situation, and
be in the cracks of life in case you trip and fall.

I will always be at your level.

And I will always be above you to pick you up.

So, if ever your memory fails,
and you suddenly forget,

turn on the light and find your shadow.
The light needs to be on to see me.

Remember: I am permanent
and so are my promises.

For my father and mother have forsaken me,
but the Lord will take me in.

- Psalm 27:10 ESV

Psalm 94:14   Psalm 121:5   Psalm 91:1

\bro.ken\

| ˈbrō-kən | adjective

1. not complete or full

\prom.ises\

| ˈprä-məs | noun

2. a reason to expect something

I promised I wouldn't fall head over heels,
that I would think with my head first and not with my
heart.

I promised if I saw red flags
I would check in with you first.

I promised I would not compromise my values—
what I deemed to be important.

I promised I wouldn't be used again,
used for my emotions, body, or my money.

I promised myself this would be the relationship,
that this was going to be the one.

I promised I wouldn't hurt myself again.
But I ended up with broken promises.

Dear Daughter,

When I make a promise, I mean it.

It will never break.
It will stand until the end of time.

So if you want to make sure your promises come true,
then consult with me first.

Include me in your thought process.
Include me so you can succeed.

Take everything to me in prayer.
And then after that, you will need to trust me.

I will change your thinking
so your thoughts will match mine.

Even if you end up breaking it,
all you have to do is come back.

We can work on a new plan
and discuss what to do differently.

Your promises will come to pass.
And that is a promise I intend to keep.

For no matter how many promises God has made, they are "Yes" in Christ. And so through him the "Amen" is spoken by us to the glory of God.

- 2 Corinthians 1:20 NIV

Psalm 89:34   Philippians 4:6   2 Peter 3:9

\ com.par.i.son\

|kəm-ˈper-ə-sən|noun

1. The act of comparing two or more people or things

I wanted to be the one—
the girl that never let him down.

I felt I was always competing with his ex—
even though she was never around.

Now that our relationship is over,
I find myself comparing yet again.

I look at my friends,
and feel as though I'm somewhat behind.

And all those people on social media?
They look happy—like, all the time.

I know we shouldn't trust
everything the Internet tells us.

But I still want to be happy.
I still want to be in love.

And it hurts,
I mean, it really hurts
because I can't see it happening now.

This comparison thing
has taken on a life of its own.

It's like the more I entertain it,
my feelings switch from envy to ice cold
heartlessness.

Speaking of social media:
his profile picture popped up on my feed.

He's with a new girl now.
Is it so bad that I wished the girl was me?

This is the life I want—wanted—with him.

He seems so happy.
She seems so happy.
I'm so unhappy when I compare myself to her.

Dear Daughter,

When you compare yourself to someone else,
you make me very sad.

I put so much thought and effort into you. I gave
you everything I had.

You can try to change your looks.

But I picked your face
and those beautiful eyes.

You can try to change your personality.

But I knew that your gentle quiet nature
would always come in handy.

And you can try to change your heart.

But I gave you a heart like mine—
a heart to remind others just how much they are
loved.

So, go ahead and try, my darling.

But your spirit knows.
And I know too.

Why not just come to me
with whatever is displeasing you?

For I have an answer for every thought
you could possibly think.

Remember I am your creator— I created you.
So, why wouldn't I have a manual on how to help
you?

I will show you how you're supposed to work. And
then you will see.

You will see you were right all along
to just simply trust me.

Before I formed you in the womb I knew
you, before you were born I set you apart; I
appointed you as a prophet to the nations.

- Jeremiah 1:5 NIV

2 Corinthians 10:12   Psalm 139:13-14   Genesis 1:27

My gifts to you...

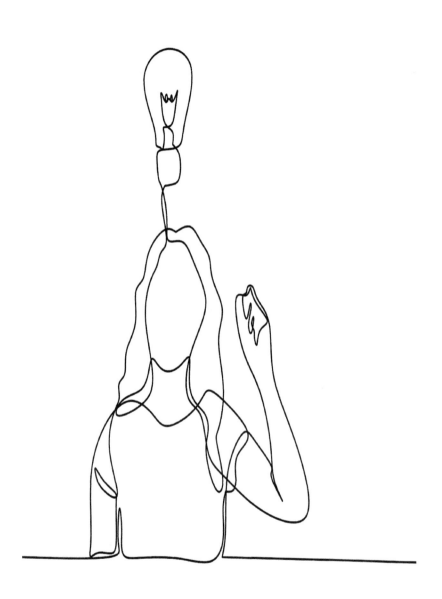

\ dis.cern.ment \

|di-ˈsərn-mənt |noun

1. The quality of being able to grasp and comprehend what is obscure; skill in discerning

Maybe I was doing it wrong.
I think I trusted way too soon.

I'm used to trusting people one hundred percent,
and then seeing if they would hurt me.

He used to ask,
"Have I done anything that would make you not trust
me?"

I answered no at the time.

But if I'm being honest,
deep down I knew the truth.

The signs were there when he failed to come
through.

So, how do I trust someone?
When my heart has been broken time and time
again?

I mean, I got it so wrong.
What if I get it wrong again?

How will I know if someone is lying?
How will I know if I'm lying to myself?

I don't think I can date someone again when I don't
even trust myself.

Dear Daughter,

I know you are second-guessing yourself because of
what happened.
But the key is to trust me and not your own ability.

You can't do this alone,
for your judgment will fail you every single time.

It can get cloudy with all the thoughts you
have going through your mind.

Let me in on what you are thinking;
let me in on your feelings, too.

I long to hear from you, my daughter.
I want to talk to you.

We need to be in constant communication
because I never want to see you go through this kind
of pain again.

I am the only one that can see the future.
So, I will let you know when it's safe to proceed.

You can trust me.
You don't have to be scared or worried.

You now have the spirit of discernment
that will never fail.

The next thing you need to receive right now
is my amazing grace.

Dear friends, do not believe every spirit, but test the spirits to see whether they are from God, because many false prophets have gone out into the world.

- 1 John 4:1 NIV

Philippians 3:3 Jeremiah 29:12-13 John 16:13

\ grace \

| ˈgrās | noun

1. a manifestation of favor

This isn't my first time.
I've been in bad relationships before.

It's like every time I think I've learned my lesson,
I find myself getting burned again.

Yes, he has a different name.
So of course, I think I wouldn't fall.
But somehow, I always trip.
And that seems to be my downfall.

Back-to-back relationships
with the same sad results.

The same mistakes being made.
Why can't I get a break from it all?

Now I sit here and wonder
how disappointed You must be.

Even now,
spending all this time with me.

I bet You're wondering—
wondering when will this girl ever learn.

What will it take for her to get it?
To get it in her head.

You must be thinking this way,
because I know I am.

Dear Daughter,

Just because you made mistakes
doesn't mean my love stops,

for there is absolutely nothing you can do
that will stop me from loving you.

So, whether you trip,
or fall,
just know my grace will always meet you.

It will catch you
and wrap you in my love.

It will not hold onto your mistakes or shortcomings
if you repent. But instead it will correct you,
because of my love.

So, don't let your mind
remind you of your past.

Let it remind you that ALL things work together for
your good.

Through me you have strength,
strength to overcome your mistakes.

All it simply takes is prayer.

the LORD make his face shine on you and be
gracious to you;

- Numbers 6:25 NIV

Jeremiah 31:32 Corinthians 12:9 Ephesians 1:7

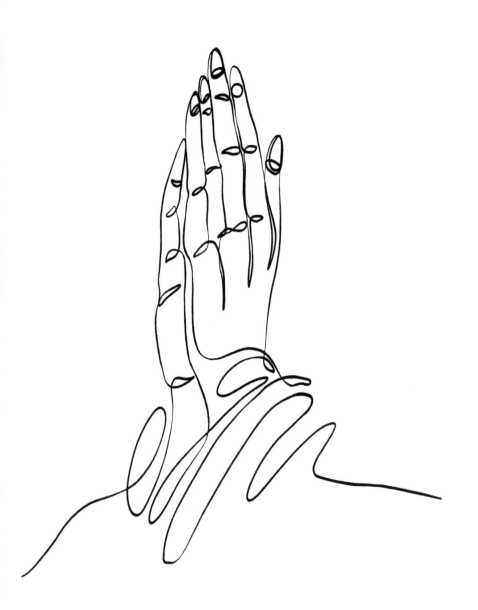

\ prayer\

| ˈprer | noun

1. a solemn request for help or expression of thanks addressed to God

I struggled with prayer
because I felt so unworthy.

I guess, deep down,
I thought You were going to judge me.

I thought if I didn't fully believe in what I was saying,
I wouldn't have to feel your disappointment
and Your anger towards me.

So, I rattled off some words
and threw them up to heaven.

Just in case You were listening.
Just in case You cared.

Until one day, I ran into trouble.
And I didn't know what to do.

But my heart knew I needed You.
And my spirit knew it too.

And even when I struggled with my words,
it seemed my spirit knew what to say.

My heart prayed and prayed and prayed.
And then You spoke to me one day.

I realized I was wrong,
and just how much prayer works,

how much You truly care about me,
especially when it hurts.

But I still feel like I'm doing it wrong.
I feel like I still don't know how to pray.

So, can You teach me, Jesus?
Teach me how to talk to you?

Teach me what to say,
and how to say
I love you?

Dear Daughter,

You've heard about the five love languages?
Well, prayer is mine.

It creates the perfect intimacy.
And it's the strongest love connector.

I desire to be close to you—
as close to you as possible.

But in order for me to do so,
I need you to share as much as possible.

Share everything that is on your mind,
and share what is in your heart too.

Keep searching for me,
and I will come to you.

Don't worry if you get tongue-tied,
or if you don't know where to start.

That's why you have the Holy Spirit,
for He knows what to say,
and He will speak on your behalf,
if you happen to struggle one day.

It is important to believe, my child,
believe the words you say,

as it is through your faith
that I move and act on your behalf.

And after you're finished speaking,
don't break our special bond.

Sit with me for a while
as I might reveal myself.

You see, prayer is not a one-way street,
but a dialogue that requires both parties.

I long to share intimate details with you,
as long as you're not in a hurry.

But if you still can't hear me,
after you've prayed,
and prayed,
and prayed…

Ask the Holy Spirit to open your eyes,
because I may still have something to say.

I may send someone to you,
to speak life into you.

I may direct you to a sermon,
to have my words preached to you.

Never discount the subtleties of the day.
I have endless ways to let you know
I hear you and I care.

But until you see me move,
it is important to thank me in prayer.

Thank me for what I'm about to do.
Thank me for your answered prayer.

For all I need is praise and faith to move on your
behalf.

Call to me and I will answer you, and will tell you great and hidden things that you have not known.

- Jeremiah 33:3 ESV

Matthew 7:7   Job 33:14   Hebrews 13:15

\ faith \

| ˈfāth | noun

1. *strong belief or trust in someone or something*

Dear Jesus,

I've always struggled with this
for as long as I can remember.

Sometimes I have it,
and sometimes I don't.

I say that I trust You,
but when a storm hits, I break.

I completely give up on You,
as my world begins to shake.

I want to take control,
and fix what is broken.

But when I try,
it seems like I only make it worse.

If only I had faith.

Faith in You to fix things
and put them back the way they're meant to be.

If only I left things in Your hands.
How much better I might be.

Teach me, Jesus.

Teach me how to keep my faith
when I just don't know what to do.

Dear Daughter,

All I require from you is faith the size of a mustard
seed.
It may not seem like a lot,
but that is truly all I need.

In time, it will grow.
In time, it will stretch.

But until then, don't beat yourself up
if it wavers every now and then.

And when you think I won't come through for you
in a crisis,
go back to the beginning
to remember why you should trust me.

Why do you believe in me?
Do you believe that I am good?

What happened the last time?
Did I not turn things around for the better?

Remember the answers to these questions.
Remember when your doubt is louder than the truth.

Remember who I am.
And then faith will come back to you.

because you know that the testing of your faith produces perseverance.

- James 1:3 NIV

Matthew 17:20   Luke 17:5   Romans 8:28

Who I am...

Who Are You?

Dear Daughter,

I am your life vest and your life craft.
I will help navigate your storms.

I am faithful and consistent.
I am your best friend. You can confide in me.

I am your counsellor and your doctor.
I know how to make things right.

I am your hope when you are hopeless.
I am your breath of fresh air and your forever light.

I am your joy and your peace.
You can forever rest in me.

I am merciful. I am forgiving.
I am good and all knowing.

I am the Author and the Finisher.
So daughter, let me write your love story.

You can put your faith in me,
because I will never let you down.

There is no one like me.
No one.

I am the great I Am.

Be still, and know that I am God; I will be exalted among the nations, I will be exalted in the earth!

- Psalm 46:10 NKJV

2 Thessalonians 3:3 Hebrews 12:2 Jeremiah 10:6

A new season...

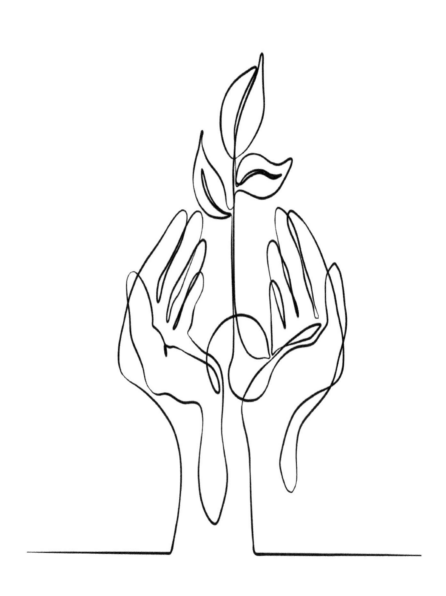

\ pur.pose\

| ˈpər-pəs | verb

1. the aim or goal of a person: what a person is trying to do, become, etc.

Why was I born?

Was I simply a mistake, or was I destined to be here?

Why do I have the kind of heart that I have?

Why do I have the kind of feelings that I do?

I want to know the answers to my questions, but who can answer them for me?

Can you answer my questions, Jesus?

I'm really tired of not knowing.

What is my purpose on this earth?

Why should I keep on going?

Dear Daughter,

I planted something
inside of you.

Something that is unique
and only for you.

It is something you may struggle with at first,
but only because you need me to fulfill it through
you.

It will help you serve others.
So it's worth living and fighting for.

It is very special to me
and this is why the enemy fights you so hard.

He will do what he can
to make sure you don't know what it is.

It is such a shame that so many people die
not knowing the gifts that I have gifted them.

And the ones that do?
The enemy will send them distractions.

But I will send you visions, dreams, and people
to keep you focused.

This is so much bigger.
Bigger than you.

There are people counting on you to walk in purpose,
waiting to hear your testimony and to be healed.

This is not to overwhelm you, my child,
this is to encourage you.

Operating in your purpose comes with so many
blessings,
more than you could even imagine.

Not sure what it is?
Then spend time with me to find out.

After your purpose is discovered,
we can build your confidence.

The LORD will fulfill his purpose for me;
your steadfast love, O LORD, endures forever.
Do not forsake the work of your hands.

- Psalm 138:8 ESV

Romans 8:28   1 Peter 4:10   Matthew 5:16

\ con.fi.dence\

| ˈkän-fə-dən(t)s | noun

1. a feeling or belief that you can do something well or succeed at something

Jesus,

I know I'm different,
but I'm worried that I'm too different.

My friends say I talk about you way too much.
But they are just worried I might throw the right
"one" off.

I tried talking to them.
I tried explaining to them my love for You,

how I wanted a different life
and how I am now living for You.

But they just don't get it.

They think that I see myself as being better than
others.
Why would they think that when all I want is what You
want for me?

This journey is so lonely.
I didn't sign up for this.

There's no one that understands me,
that understands what's going on in my heart and in
my head.

Sometimes I wish
I could just go back to my old life.

But I know that would be pretending
and living a lie.

But am I really who You say I am, Jesus?
Maybe You got it all wrong.

Why do I feel more uncomfortable now
than I ever have before?

What if I never get to where You expect me to be?
Can I really be all who You have called me to be?

Maybe it's all just a mistake.
Maybe You got the wrong one.

Dear Daughter,

You were made to be different, my darling,
different from all the rest.

Don't worry about what others think about you.
Focus on hearing my voice instead.

People will laugh at you, and
tell you that what you believe doesn't make sense.

They will say you're not talented enough,
but I need you to rise above that.

You have a new identity, my daughter,
one that no longer fits the old you.

The things you were once attracted to
will no longer attract you.

I can understand your doubts,
and see why you would question your calling.

But I have already given you everything
you need to accomplish your calling.

Just reach out and claim it.
Positive thinking will help you accomplish this
through faith.

And no, I did not make a mistake, my darling,
because you were already destined for greatness.

I will send you intentional friends,
friends that may not get your purpose, but that will
get you.

You will also meet people walking in their purpose.
They will speak and relate to you.

And then there will be the "one"—
the one that will understand you, understand your
heart.

I know you want him to come now,
but there is still more work to be done.

for the Lord will be your confidence and will keep your foot from being caught.

- Proverbs 3:26 ESV

John 10:27   Matthew 5:11   Psalm 71:21

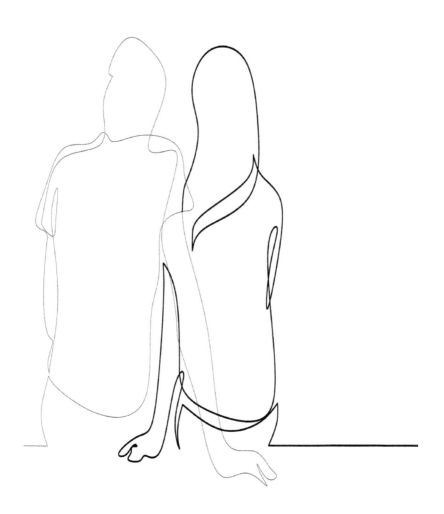

\ single.ness \
| ˈsiŋ-gəl-nəs | noun

*2. the quality or state of being single;
not having or including another*

Okay, I have done this single thing for a while now.
But why aren't guys approaching me?

It feels as though there
is something wrong with me.

We've worked on me.
And worked, and worked, and worked…

But I feel like somehow, it's worked against me.

My standards must be too high.
What else can it be?

I think I'm ready.
I mean, I know I'm ready.

So then, where is he?

Where is the man I have been waiting for?

I'm tempted to go back,
back to what I'm used to.

But I know that would be settling.

So, how much longer?
It's been a few years.

Did You forget about me, Jesus?
Once again?

Dear Daughter,

Your singleness was never meant to be a life sentence, but there are some things I still need to teach you.

Why would you want to rush this process? Why can't I just spend some quality time with you?

I know you feel like you are healed and ready to find your prince charming.

But let's not forget everything I've shown you when it comes to your purpose.

Continue to follow my directions.
Continue to listen to my voice.

You will see once you are in my will, the feeling of needing someone—a relationship—will vanish.

For I am the only One who can truly fill that void.

Yes, it gets lonely.
It may feel like you've been forgotten.

But if you remain in me, you will know when the time is right.

So, until then, darling, it's okay to wait.

Remember what I told you from the very beginning:
I have an obligation to protect you.
So, let me do my job.

You are covered until I say you are ready.
You may not thank me right now,
but I know one day you will.

Delight yourself in the LORD, and he will give you the desires of your heart.

- Psalm 37:4 ESV

Lamentations 3:25-26 Isaiah 58:11 Proverbs 3:5-6

My best...

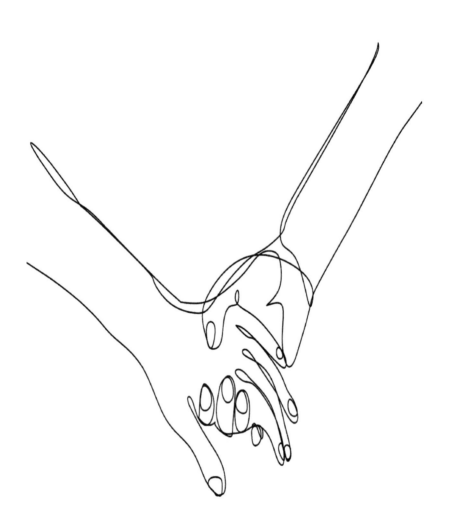

(His) \ best \
| 'best | adjective

1. better than all others in quality or value

Dear Daughter,

When the time is right,
I will send you my best.

My best will not be perfect,
but he will be unlike all the rest.

You will know he is my best by the fruit that he produces,
like patience and kindness.
Yes, he will know how to treat, honor, and respect you.

He will pray with you, and for you.
And be your protector on this Earth.

He will see you and
accept you—mistakes and all.

And when things get a little rocky,
and he's unsure what to do,
he will seek me first
and then will come find you.

Lastly, he will support your purpose
and be a part of your purpose too.

Because you see,
this partnership is much bigger than the two of you.

So, yes, daughter, my best will know how to love you.
He will know what you need.

And He will have that love to give you,
because he first loved me.

226

And we know that God causes everything to work together for the good of those who love God and are called according to his purpose for them

- Romans 8:28 NLT

Ecclesiastes 3:1   John 15:13   Matthew 22:37

Epilogue

Dear Heavenly Father,

Thank you, for holding on to my hand as you led me on this healing journey. After seeing my true reflection, I understand just how important it is to view myself through your eyes.

Thank you for your wisdom, love, and encouragement and for piecing me back together again. Thank you for breaking the strongholds over my life and for setting me free—once and for all.

I know this journey is far from over. But I am confident that I will get through it with your help. I am committed to getting to know more about you by reading your word day and night.

I declare happiness, peace, joy, and love over my life today and forever more.

In Jesus' mighty name, amen.

Acknowledgments

Thank you, God, for being with me through one of the most difficult heartbreaks I have ever experienced. Thank you so much for never leaving my side, and for guiding me on the right path for healing. I am forever grateful for I now know my worth and my purpose. I am nothing without you, and give you all the glory for this book.

My sister, Renee, who has been my therapist and best friend.

My friends that have never switched. Thank you to my solid group of friends (extended family included), who have supported me through my breakup, and have listened to me re-tell this story from hurt to purpose.

My Brave By Faith 2019 Israel Sisterhood—God knew I needed friends that understood my heart. He knew I needed you. I will never forget the time that we shared, and our girl's night when the topic of my book came up. Thank you, Aly! You guys have inspired me more than you could ever know.

To everyone that has allowed me to share my story before this book was even in existence, and to those who have suggested ideas with piecing it all together—your input, feedback, and just being there for me as I vented or when I needed encouragement means the world to me.

To the team at Lincross Publishing.

To my parents who dragged me to church every Sunday, until I was old enough to make the decision on my own (and encouraging me on days when I didn't feel like going).

And last, but not least, to my future husband—thank you for reading my book. Thank you for accepting my past. And for loving all of me.

Love,

Tonya

Notes

1. Merriam-Webster, s.v. "daughter" accessed September 19th, 2020. https://www.merriam-webster.com/dictionary/daughter

2. National Coalition Against Domestic Violence (2015). Facts about domestic violence and psychological abuse. Retrieved from www.ncadv.org (https://assets.speakcdn.com/assets/2497/domestic_violence_and_psychological_abuse_ncadv.pdf)

3. National Domestic Violence Hotline. Get The Facts & Figures (https://www.thehotline.org/resources/statistics/)

4. Government of Canada (2018). Family violence: How big is the problem in Canada? (https://www.canada.ca/en/public-health/services/health-promotion/stop-family-violence/problem-canada.html)

5. Merriam-Webster, s.v. "confused" accessed September 19, 2020. https://www.merriam-webster.com/dictionary/confused

6. Merriam-Webster, s.v. "worthless" accessed September 19, 2020. https://www.dictionary.com/browse/worthless

7. Merriam-Webster, s.v. "alone" accessed September 19, 2020. https://www.dictionary.com/browse/alone

8. Merriam-Webster, s.v. "blame" accessed September 19, 2020. https://www.dictionary.com/browse/blame

9. Merriam-Webster, s.v. "soul" accessed September 19, 2020. https://www.dictionary.com/browse/soul

10. Merriam-Webster, s.v. "tie" accessed September 19, 2020. https://www.dictionary.com/browse/tie

11. Merriam-Webster, s.v. "goodbye" accessed September 19, 2020. https://www.merriam-webster. com/dictionary/goodbye

12. Lexico.com/Oxford dictionaries, s.v. "ashamed" accessed September 19, 2020. https://www.lexico. com/definition/ashamed

13. Dictionary.com, s.v. "anger" accessed September 19, 2020. https://www.dictionary.com/browse/anger

14. Merriam-Webster, s.v. "self-medication" accessed September 19, 2020. https://www.merriam-webster. com/dictionary/self-medication

15. Merriam-Webster, s.v. "forgiveness" accessed September 19, 2020. https://www.merriam-webster. com/dictionary/forgiveness

16. Merriam-Webster, s.v. "love" accessed September 19, 2020. https://www.merriam-webster.com/ dictionary/love

17. Merriam-Webster, s.v. "healing" accessed September 19, 2020.

18. Merriam-Webster, s.v. "promised" accessed September 19, 2020. https://www.merriam-webster. com/dictionary/promised

19. In Lexico.com/Oxford dictionaries, s.v. "mask" accessed September 19, 2020. https://www.lexico. com/definition/mask

20. Dictionary.com, s.v. "truth" accessed September 19, 2020. https://www.dictionary.com/browse/truth

21. Dictionary.com, s.v. "identity" accessed September 19, 2020. https://www.dictionary.com/browse/identity

22. Lexico.com/Oxford dictionaries, s.v. "strength" accessed September 19, 2020. https://www.lexico.com/definition/strength

23. Merriam-Webster, s.v. "renewed" accessed September 19, 2020. https://www.merriam-webster.com/dictionary/renewed

24. Dictionary.Cambridge.org, s.v. "rejection" accessed September 19, 2020. https://dictionary.cambridge.org/dictionary/english/rejection

25. Dictionary.Cambridge.org, s.v. "anxiety" accessed September 19, 2020. https://dictionary.cambridge.org/dictionary/english/anxiety

26. Merriam-Webster, s.v. "co-dependency" accessed September 19, 2020. https://www.merriam-webster.com/dictionary/codependency

27. Merriam-Webster, s.v. "peace" accessed September 19, 2020. https://www.merriam-webster.com/dictionary/peace

28. Dictionary.Cambridge.org, s.v. "abandonment" accessed September 19, 2020.28. https://dictionary.cambridge.org/dictionary/english/abandonment

29. Merriam-Webster, s.v. "broken" accessed September 19, 2020. https://www.merriam-webster.com/dictionary/broken

30. Merriam-Webster, s.v. "promises" accessed September 19, 2020. https://www.merriam-webster.com/dictionary/promises

31. Dictionary.Cambridge.org, s.v. "comparison" accessed September 19, 2020. https://dictionary. cambridge.org/dictionary/english/comparison

32. Merriam-Webster, s.v. "discernment" accessed September 19, 2020. https://www.merriam-webster. com/dictionary/discernment

33. Dictionary.com, s.v. "grace" accessed September 19, 2020. https://www.dictionary.com/browse/grace

34. Lexico.com/Oxford Dictionaries, s.v. "prayer" accessed September 19, 2020. https://www.lexico. com/definition/prayer

35. Merriam-Webster, s.v. "faith" accessed September 19, 2020. https://www.merriam-webster.com/ dictionary/faith

36. Merriam-Webster, s.v. "purpose" accessed September 19, 2020. https://www.merriam-webster. com/dictionary/purpose

37. Merriam-Webster, s.v. "confidence" accessed September 19, 2020. https://www.merriam-webster. com/dictionary/confidence

38. Merriam-Webster, s.v. "singleness" accessed September 19, 2020. https://www.merriam-webster. com/dictionary/singleness

39. Merriam-Webster, s.v. "best" accessed September 19, 2020. https://www.merriam-webster.com/ dictionary/best

About the Author

Tonya Raymond is a writer based in Toronto, Canada. She is also a self-love coach, specializing in helping women who have come out of an unhealthy relationship or are still struggling in some aspect of their healing journey. As a result, Tonya started an online community called Dear God's Daughter to teach women self-love through God's eyes.

In 2019, Tonya decided to Google her name, and came across a biblical meaning from grandmahelenshouse.com.

The name Tonya means 'of highest worth or praise'. Then Tonya would be 'of great value to the Lord'… This is the job He has given Tonya— to show others their worth to the Lord. There are many who feel that they are worthless and that there is no purpose for them here on this earth. Tonya, coming from the presence of the Lord, can assure them that this is not true. Those that have been in the presence of the Lord can testify of His great love. Tonya can do this, for this is where her spirit resides. Luke 12:7 But even the very hairs of your head are all numbered. Fear not therefore: ye are of more value than many sparrows.

Tonya truly believes this is her purpose. She is forever grateful that she trusted God in seeing this through.

To be a part of everything God has laid out in her heart, visit Tonya's website and subscribe to the mailing list!

Website: deargodsdaughter.com
Instagram: @deargodsdaughter
Email: hello@deargodsdaughter.com
Download your free workbook: visit deargodsdaughter.com

Printed in the USA
CPSIA information can be obtained
at www.ICGtesting.com
LVHW020549190724
785912LV00020B/95